COOKING WITH GRAPES

GRAPES

50 DELICIOUS GRAPE RECIPES

By
Chef Maggie Chow

Published by
BookSumo, a division of Saxonberg Associates
http://www.booksumo.com/

INTRODUCTION

Welcome to *The Effortless Chef Series*! Thank you for taking the time to download *Cooking with Grapes*. Come take a journey with me into the delights of easy cooking. The point of this cookbook and all my cookbooks is to exemplify the effortless nature of cooking simply.

In this book we focus on Cooking with Grapes. You will find that even though the recipes are simple, the taste of the dishes is quite amazing.

So will you join me in an adventure of simple cooking? If the answer is yes (and I hope it is) please consult the table of contents to find the dishes you are most interested in. Once you are ready jump right in and start cooking.

— Chef Maggie Chow

TABLE OF CONTENTS

ANY ISSUES? CONTACT ME

If you find that something important to you is missing from this book please contact me at maggie@booksumo.com.

I will try my best to re-publish a revised copy taking your feedback into consideration and let you know when the book has been revised with you in mind.

:)

— Chef Maggie Chow

LEGAL NOTES

Common Abbreviations

cup(s)	C.
tablespoon	tbsp
teaspoon	tsp
ounce	oz.
pound	lb

*All units used are standard American measurements

Chapter 1: Easy Grape Recipes

Holiday Special Creamy Grapes

Ingredients

- 4 lb. seedless grapes, stemmed
- 1 C. sour cream
- 1 (8 oz.) package cream cheese
- 1/2 C. white sugar
- 1 tsp vanilla extract

Directions

- Rinse the grapes and pat them dry with a paper towel.
- In a large bowl, add the remaining ingredients and mix till well combined.
- Fold in the grapes and refrigerate to chill overnight.

Amount per serving (12 total)

Timing Information:

Preparation	20 m
Cooking	8 h 20 m
Total Time	8 h 40 m

Nutritional Information:

Calories	247 kcal
Fat	11.4 g
Carbohydrates	36.6g
Protein	3 g
Cholesterol	29 mg
Sodium	68 mg

* Percent Daily Values are based on a 2,000 calorie diet.

WONDERFULLY REFRESHING GRAPES

Ingredients

- 1 C. heavy whipping cream
- 1 C. granular no-calorie sucralose sweetener
- 1 C. plain yogurt
- 1 (8 oz.) package cream cheese, softened
- 1 tsp almond extract
- 1 tsp vanilla extract
- 1 1/2 lb. seedless green grapes
- 1 1/2 lb. seedless red grapes

Directions

- In a glass bowl, add the whipping cream and beat till foamy.
- Slowly, add the sweetener, beating continuously till medium peaks form.
- Add the cream cheese, yogurt, vanilla and almond extract and beat till well combined.
- Fold in the grapes and refrigerate to chill for about 1 hour.

Amount per serving (12 total)

Timing Information:

Preparation	15 m
Cooking	1 h 15 m
Total Time	1 h 30 m

Nutritional Information:

Calories	236 kcal
Fat	14.8 g
Carbohydrates	24.5g
Protein	3.6 g
Cholesterol	49 mg
Sodium	79 mg

* Percent Daily Values are based on a 2,000 calorie diet.

CLASSIC GRAPE JELLY

Ingredients

- 3 C. grape juice
- 5 1/4 C. white sugar
- 1 (2 oz.) package powdered fruit pectin

Directions

- Sterilize the jars, then dry them completely and keep aside.
- In a large pan, mix together the pectin and grape juice on medium-high heat.
- Bring to a boil and boil, stirring continuously, for about 1 minute.
- Add the sugar and stir till it is dissolved completely.
- Remove everything from the heat and transfer the jelly into jars, leaving about 1/2-inch space from the top.
- Cover the jars with the lids and seal tightly.
- Keep everything at room temperature for about 24 hours.
- Refrigerate to set for about 7 days before serving.
- This jelly can be stored in refrigerator for about 3 weeks.

Amount per serving (48 total)

Timing Information:

Preparation	5 m
Cooking	15 m
Total Time	20 m

Nutritional Information:

Calories	94 kcal
Fat	0 g
Carbohydrates	24.2g
Protein	0.1 g
Cholesterol	0 mg
Sodium	1 mg

* Percent Daily Values are based on a 2,000 calorie diet.

REFRESHING GRAPE SHERBET

Ingredients

- 1 (14 oz.) can sweetened condensed milk
- 2 C. heavy cream
- 3 C. white sugar
- 4 C. grape juice
- 3 lemons, juiced
- whole milk

Directions

- In a large container of an ice-cream machine, add all the ingredients except milk and stir to combine.
- Add enough milk so that it reaches the fill line of the container.
- Process according to the manufacturer's directions.

Amount per serving (32 total)

Timing Information:

Preparation	20 m
Cooking	50 m
Total Time	1 h 10 m

Nutritional Information:

Calories	203 kcal
Fat	7.6 g
Carbohydrates	33g
Protein	2.6 g
Cholesterol	28 mg
Sodium	35 mg

* Percent Daily Values are based on a 2,000 calorie diet.

Gorgeous Pickled Grapes

Ingredients

- 1 lb. seedless red grapes, stemmed
- 1 1/2 C. apple cider vinegar
- 1 C. water
- 1 C. raw sugar
- 1/2 small red onion, cut into slivers
- 2 tsp yellow mustard seeds
- 1 tsp whole black peppercorns
- 1 cinnamon stick
- 1 bay leaf
- 1 star anise pod
- 1 whole allspice

Directions

- In a large mason jar, add the grapes and keep aside.
- In a pan, mix together the remaining ingredients and bring to a boil.
- Reduce the heat to low and simmer for about 10 minutes.
- Remove everything from the heat and keep aside to cool for about 15 minutes.

- Add the spice mixture over the grapes and tightly cover with a lid.
- Gently shake the jar to combine the grapes with the spice mixture.
- Refrigerate for about 1 day before serving.

Amount per serving (10 total)

Timing Information:

Preparation	15 m
Cooking	10 m
Total Time	1 d 40 m

Nutritional Information:

Calories	120 kcal
Fat	0.5 g
Carbohydrates	28.4g
Protein	0.6 g
Cholesterol	0 mg
Sodium	11 mg

* Percent Daily Values are based on a 2,000 calorie diet.

BURNT GRAPES

Ingredients

- 2 C. sour cream
- 1/2 C. confectioners' sugar
- 2 h vanilla extract
- 5 C. green seedless grapes
- 1 C. butter
- 1 C. brown sugar

Directions

- In a large bowl, add the confectioners' sugar, sour cream and vanilla extract and mix till well combined.
- Fold in the grapes.
- In a pan, melt the butter and brown sugar on medium heat.
- Cook, stirring continuously till a thick mixture forms.
- Place the butter mixture over the grape mixture and gently, stir to combine.
- Refrigerate to chill for about 1-2 hours.

Amount per serving (12 total)

Timing Information:

Preparation	5 m
Cooking	10 m
Total Time	2 h 15 m

Nutritional Information:

Calories	337 kcal
Fat	23.8 g
Carbohydrates	30.8g
Protein	1.8 g
Cholesterol	58 mg
Sodium	134 mg

* Percent Daily Values are based on a 2,000 calorie diet.

SWEET & SPICY GRAPES CHINESE STYLE

Ingredients

- 1/2 C. white sugar
- 1/2 C. water
- 1/2 tsp Chinese five-spice powder
- 1 lb. seedless grapes

Directions

- In a pan, mix together the water and sugar on medium heat and cook, stirring, till the sugar dissolves.
- Remove everything from the heat and stir in the five-spice powder.
- With a fork, pierce the grapes and add into a sealable bag with the sugar mixture.
- Seal the bag tightly and shake well.
- Refrigerate for about 24 hours, flipping occasionally.

Amount per serving (12 total)

Timing Information:

Preparation	10 m
Cooking	5 m
Total Time	1 d 15 m

Nutritional Information:

Calories	59 kcal
Fat	0.2 g
Carbohydrates	15.1g
Protein	0.3 g
Cholesterol	0 mg
Sodium	1 mg

* Percent Daily Values are based on a 2,000 calorie diet.

ELEGANT GRAPE TREAT

Ingredients

- 2 lb. red seedless grapes, stemmed
- 1 (3 oz.) package cherry flavored Jell-O mix

Directions

- In a shallow dish, place the Jello-o mix.
- Coat the grapes with the Jello-o mix generously.
- Place the coated grapes in a serving bowl and refrigerate for about 1 hour.

Amount per serving (8 total)

Timing Information:

Preparation	5 m
Cooking	1 h 5 m
Total Time	1 h 20 m

Nutritional Information:

Calories	119 kcal
Fat	0.7 g
Carbohydrates	29.2g
Protein	1.7 g
Cholesterol	0 mg
Sodium	50 mg

* Percent Daily Values are based on a 2,000 calorie diet.

POTLUCK GRAPE SALAD

Ingredients

- 1 lb. seedless green grapes, stemmed
- 1 lb. seedless red grapes, stemmed
- 1 (8 oz.) package cream cheese, softened
- 1 (7 oz.) jar marshmallow crème
- 1 (6 oz.) package slivered almonds

Directions

- In a bowl, add the marshmallow crème and cream cheese and mix till creamy and smooth.
- Add the grapes and almonds and gently, stir to combine.
- Serve immediately or refrigerate covered for about 1 hour.

Amount per serving (8 total)

Timing Information:

Preparation	15 m
Cooking	1 h 15 m
Total Time	1 h 30 m

Nutritional Information:

Calories	385 kcal
Fat	21.2 g
Carbohydrates	44.4g
Protein	7.4 g
Cholesterol	31 mg
Sodium	107 mg

* Percent Daily Values are based on a 2,000 calorie diet.

CREAMY GRAPES FRENCH STYLE II

Ingredients

- 5 oz. almonds
- 1/2 (8 oz.) package cream cheese, softened
- 1 (3 oz.) package Roquefort cheese
- 1 1/2 tbsp heavy cream
- 1/4 lb. seedless red grapes
- 1/4 lb. seedless green grapes

Directions

- Set your oven to 375 degrees F before doing anything else.
- Arrange the almonds onto a baking sheet in a single layer and cook everything in the oven for about 5-10 minutes, stirring occasionally.
- In a food processor, add the toasted almonds and pulse till chopped roughly, then transfer into a shallow dish.
- In a bowl, add the heavy cream, Roquefort cheese and cream cheese and beat till creamy and smooth.
- Add the grapes and gently, stir to combine then coat everything with the almonds evenly.

- Transfer the grapes onto a wax paper lined plate and refrigerate before serving.

Amount per serving (6 total)

Timing Information:

Preparation	30 m
Cooking	10 m
Total Time	40 m

Nutritional Information:

Calories	292 kcal
Fat	24.3 g
Carbohydrates	12.2g
Protein	9.7 g
Cholesterol	38 mg
Sodium	314 mg

* Percent Daily Values are based on a 2,000 calorie diet.

Harvest Time Grape Pie

Ingredients

- 4 1/2 C. Concord grapes
- 1 C. white sugar
- 1/4 C. all-purpose flour
- 2 tsp lemon juice
- 1/8 tsp salt
- 1 (9 inch) pie shell
- 1/2 C. quick cooking oats
- 1/2 C. packed brown sugar
- 1/4 C. all-purpose flour
- 1/4 C. butter

Directions

- Set your oven to 425 degrees F before doing anything else and arrange a sheet pan on the lower rack of the oven.
- Carefully, remove the skin from the pulp by squeezing the end of the grapes.
- Reserve the skin of the grapes.

- In a pan, add the grape pulp and bring to a gentle simmer and cook, stirring continuously for about 1 minute.
- Transfer the cooked pulp in a strainer and with a spoon, press to remove the seeds.
- In a bowl, mix together the pulp, skin, 1/4 cup of the flour, sugar, salt and lime juice.
- Place the grape mixture into the pie shell evenly.
- In another bowl, mix together the remaining flour, oats, and brown sugar.
- With a pastry cutter, cut the butter and mix till a crumbly mixture forms.
- Place the oat mixture over the filling mixture evenly.
- With some foil, cover the sides of the pastry and arrange in the sheet pan.
- Cook everything in the oven for about 15 minutes.
- Remove the foil paper and cook for about 20 minutes more.

Timing Information:

Preparation	1 h
Cooking	35 m
Total Time	5 h 35 m

Nutritional Information:

Calories	203 kcal
Fat	7.6 g
Carbohydrates	33g
Protein	2.6 g
Cholesterol	28 mg
Sodium	35 mg

* Percent Daily Values are based on a 2,000 calorie diet.

Fabulous Party Salsa

Ingredients

- 1 1/2 C. seedless red grapes, chopped
- 1 avocado - peeled, pitted and diced
- 1/4 C. chopped red bell pepper
- 2 tbsp chopped yellow bell pepper
- 2 tbsp chopped sweet onion
- 2 tbsp chopped fresh cilantro
- 1 tbsp lime juice
- 1/2 tsp garlic salt
- 1 pinch ground black pepper

Directions

- In a large bowl, mix together all the ingredients.
- Refrigerate for about 30 minutes before serving.

Amount per serving (8 total)

Timing Information:

Preparation	1 h
Cooking	35 m
Total Time	5 h 35 m

Nutritional Information:

Calories	66 kcal
Fat	3.9 g
Carbohydrates	8.4g
Protein	0.8 g
Cholesterol	0 mg
Sodium	116 mg

* Percent Daily Values are based on a 2,000 calorie diet.

Heavenly Yummy Grapes Snack

Ingredients

- 2 C. white chocolate chips
- 2 tsp shortening
- 1 lb. seedless grapes
- 1 C. finely chopped salted peanuts

Directions

- In a microwave safe bowl, add the shortening and white chocolate chips and microwave on high, stirring after every 30 seconds till smooth.
- On a wax paper lined plate, place the chopped peanuts.
- Dip the grapes into the melted chocolate mixture, then coat with the chopped peanuts.
- Transfer the grapes onto a wax paper lined plate and keep aside to set.

Amount per serving (20 total)

Timing Information:

Preparation	20 m
Cooking	2 m
Total Time	22 m

Nutritional Information:

Calories	163 kcal
Fat	10.5 g
Carbohydrates	15.7g
Protein	3.1 g
Cholesterol	4 mg
Sodium	77 mg

* Percent Daily Values are based on a 2,000 calorie diet.

LUNCHTIME GRAPE WRAPS

Ingredients

- 4 C. chopped cooked turkey
- 2 C. red seedless grapes, halved
- 1/2 C. grated Parmesan cheese
- 1/2 C. mayonnaise
- salt and ground black pepper to taste
- 4 (8 inch) flour tortillas
- 4 large fresh spinach leaves

Directions

- In a bowl, add the grapes, turkey, mayonnaise, Parmesan, salt and black pepper and gently, mix to combine.
- Place 1 spinach leaf in the middle of each tortilla and divide the grape mixture over the spinach.
- Fold the bottom of each tortilla and wrap tightly to secure the filling.

Amount per serving (4 total)

Timing Information:

Preparation	15 m
Cooking	15 m
Total Time	30 m

Nutritional Information:

Calories	697 kcal
Fat	35.6 g
Carbohydrates	43.1g
Protein	50.2 g
Cholesterol	1126 mg
Sodium	748 mg

* Percent Daily Values are based on a 2,000 calorie diet.

Christmas Jellied Meatballs

Ingredients

- 2 (12 oz.) bottles Heinz Chili Sauce
- 1 (32 oz.) jars grape jelly
- 1 pinch cayenne pepper
- 3 (5 lb) bags frozen cocktail meatballs

Directions

- In a pan, mix together all the ingredients except the meatballs and cook till just warmed.
- In a crockpot, place the meatballs and top with the sauce mixture.
- Set the crockpot on low and cook, covered for about 3-4 hours.

Amount per serving: 12

Timing Information:

Preparation	5 mins
Total Time	3 hrs 5 mins

Nutritional Information:

Calories	257.5
Fat	0.1g
Cholesterol	0.0mg
Sodium	781.0mg
Carbohydrates	63.4g
Protein	1.5g

* Percent Daily Values are based on a 2,000 calorie diet.

GRAPE TREAT FOR FAMILY FUNCTIONS

Ingredients

- 1 (3 oz.) packages cream cheese
- 1 tbsp mayonnaise
- 1 tbsp sugar
- 1 dash cayenne pepper
- 1 1/2 dashes garlic powder
- 2 -3 C. green grapes, halved
- 1 C. chopped pecans

Directions

- In a bowl, add all the ingredients except the grapes and pecans and mix till well combined.
- Fold in the grapes and pecans.
- Refrigerate for about 2 hours before serving.

Amount per serving: 4

Timing Information:

Preparation	10 mins
Total Time	10 mins

Nutritional Information:

Calories	345.1
Fat	28.3g
Cholesterol	24.3mg
Sodium	90.7mg
Carbohydrates	23.0g
Protein	4.7g

* Percent Daily Values are based on a 2,000 calorie diet.

Grape Muffins for a Sweet Day

Ingredients

- 2 1/2 C. flour
- 1 C. sugar
- 2 1/2 tsp baking powder
- 1 C. milk
- 1 tsp vanilla
- 2 eggs, well beaten
- 1/2 C. butter, melted
- 1 1/2 C. red seedless grapes, cut into pieces

Directions

- Set your oven to 375 degrees F before doing anything else and line 12 cups of a muffin tin with paper liners.
- In a large bowl, mix together the flour, baking powder and sugar.
- Make a well in the center of the flour mixture and add the eggs, milk, butter and vanilla and mix till well combined.
- Fold in the grapes and transfer the mixture into prepared muffin cups.
- Cook everything in the oven for about 25 minutes.

Amount per serving: 12

Timing Information:

Preparation	15 mins
Total Time	40 mins

Nutritional Information:

Calories	266.5
Fat	9.4g
Cholesterol	54.1mg
Sodium	166.0mg
Carbohydrates	41.2g
Protein	4.6g

* Percent Daily Values are based on a 2,000 calorie diet.

SWEET GRAPES PERSIAN STYLE

Ingredients

- 1 1/2 C. red seedless grapes, cut in half
- 1 (16 oz.) containers low-fat vanilla yogurt
- 1/4 C. plus 2 tbsp firmly packed brown sugar

Directions

- In 6 serving cups, divide the grapes and top with the yogurt evenly.
- Sprinkle with the brown sugar evenly.
- Refrigerate to chill completely before serving.

Amount per serving: 6

Timing Information:

Preparation	10 mins
Total Time	10 mins

Nutritional Information:

Calories	89.2
Fat	0.4g
Cholesterol	1.6mg
Sodium	25.3mg
Carbohydrates	20.4g
Protein	1.9g

* Percent Daily Values are based on a 2,000 calorie diet.

FRENCH GRAPE TREAT

Ingredients

- 1 C. green grape, halved lengthwise
- 2 tbsp fat free sour cream
- 1 tbsp packed brown sugar

Directions

- In a bowl, mix together the sour cream and brown sugar.
- Gently, fold in the grapes.
- Serve immediately.

Amount per serving: 2

Timing Information:

Preparation	5 mins
Total Time	5 mins

Nutritional Information:

Calories	92.8
Fat	0.3g
Cholesterol	1.4mg
Sodium	14.9mg
Carbohydrates	22.8g
Protein	1.3g

* Percent Daily Values are based on a 2,000 calorie diet.

Grape Nut Pudding New England Style

Ingredients

- 5 C. milk
- 4 eggs
- 11 tbsp sugar
- 1 tsp vanilla
- 1/4 tsp salt
- 1/2 C. Post Grape-Nuts cereal

Directions

- Set your oven to 350 degrees F before doing anything else.
- In a bowl, add all the ingredients and with a hand beater, beat till well combined.
- Transfer the mixture into a 12x9-inch baking dish and Cook everything in the oven for about 1 hour.

Amount per serving: 1

Timing Information:

Preparation	1 min
Total Time	2 mins

Nutritional Information:

Calories	324.0
Fat	4.0g
Cholesterol	11.3mg
Sodium	394.4mg
Carbohydrates	68.2g
Protein	8.9g

* Percent Daily Values are based on a 2,000 calorie diet.

AMERICAN FROZEN GRAPES

Ingredients

- 36 green grapes, washed and dried
- 1 tbsp confectioners' sugar, for dusting

Directions

- In a large glass baking dish, place the dried grapes in a single layer and sprinkle with the confectioner's sugar.
- Keep the dish in the freezer till frozen.

Amount per serving: 2

Timing Information:

Preparation	1 min
Total Time	1 min

Nutritional Information:

Calories	1580.4
Fat	3.6g
Cholesterol	0.0mg
Sodium	45.4mg
Carbohydrates	414.5g
Protein	16.3g

* Percent Daily Values are based on a 2,000 calorie diet.

HEALTHY GRAPE-NUT CEREAL

Ingredients

- 1/2 C. Grape-nuts cereal
- 1/3 C. milk
- 1 tbsp honey

Directions

- In a microwave safe bowl, mix together the grape-nut cereal and milk and drizzle with the honey.
- Microwave on the high for about 30-60 seconds.

Amount per serving: 1

Timing Information:

Preparation	1 min
Total Time	2 mins

Nutritional Information:

Calories	324.0
Fat	4.0g
Cholesterol	11.3mg
Sodium	394.4mg
Carbohydrates	68.2g
Protein	8.9g

* Percent Daily Values are based on a 2,000 calorie diet.

BEST TASTING GRAPE JUICE

Ingredients

- 2 Sterilized quart jars
- 2 C. washed and cleaned concord grapes
- 1/2 C. sugar

Directions

- In sterilized jars, add and divided the grapes and sugar and enough boiling water to fill each jar.
- Immediately, seal the jar tightly with a lid.
- Process in the water bath canner for about 10 minutes.
- Remove everything from the canner and wrap with a towel and keep aside for 1 day.
- Keep aside for about 3-4 weeks before using.
- Through a strainer, strain the juice and serve.

Amount per serving: 1

Timing Information:

Preparation	30 mins
Total Time	30 mins

Nutritional Information:

Calories	510.2
Fat	0.6g
Cholesterol	0.0mg
Sodium	4.6mg
Carbohydrates	131.5g
Protein	1.1g

* Percent Daily Values are based on a 2,000 calorie diet.

GREEK GRILLED GRAPES

Ingredients

- 1 small cluster red seedless grapes
- 1/2 tsp olive oil

Directions

- Set your grill to medium-high heat.
- In a bowl, add the grape cluster and oil and toss to coat well.
- Cover and cook on grill for about 3-4 minutes.

Amount per serving: 1

Timing Information:

Preparation	1 min
Total Time	5 mins

Nutritional Information:

Calories	106.8
Fat	2.4g
Cholesterol	0.0mg
Sodium	2.5mg
Carbohydrates	22.8g
Protein	0.9g

* Percent Daily Values are based on a 2,000 calorie diet.

ENERGETIC GRAPE-NUT BARS

Ingredients

- 1 C. light corn syrup
- 1 C. sugar
- 3/4 C. peanut butter
- 4 C. Grape-nuts cereal

Directions

- In a microwave safe bowl, mix together the peanut butter, corn syrup and sugar.
- Microwave on the high for about 2 1/2 minutes, stirring after every 1 minute.
- Add the grape-nut cereal and stir to combine well.
- Transfer the mixture into a lightly greased 13x9-inch baking dish and with the back of a spatula, press downwards to smooth the surface.
- Keep aside to cool completely.
- Cut into desired size bars and serve.

Amount per serving: 1

Timing Information:

Preparation	5 mins
Total Time	10 mins

Nutritional Information:

Calories	151.4
Fat	3.5g
Cholesterol	0.0mg
Sodium	131.0mg
Carbohydrates	29.2g
Protein	3.2g

* Percent Daily Values are based on a 2,000 calorie diet.

CRUNCHY GRAPES

Ingredients

- 1 bunch green grapes
- 2 egg whites, beaten
- 1/2 C. sugar

Directions

- Coat the grapes with the beaten egg whites evenly and place in a large glass baking dish in a single layer.
- Sprinkle with sugar.
- Keep everything in freezer till frozen.

Amount per serving: 3

Timing Information:

Preparation	15 mins
Total Time	15 mins

Nutritional Information:

Calories	140.4
Fat	0.0g
Cholesterol	0.0mg
Sodium	36.5mg
Carbohydrates	33.4g
Protein	2.4g

* Percent Daily Values are based on a 2,000 calorie diet.

AMERICAN GRAPE SODA

Ingredients

- 1 1/4 C. red seedless grapes
- 1/4 C. mint leaf, lightly packed
- 1/4 C. sugar
- 1/4 C. lime juice
- 1 tsp fresh ginger, finely grated
- ice
- 1 1/2 C. soda water

Directions

- In a blender, add the grapes, sugar and mint and pulse on high for about 10 seconds.
- Add the ginger and lime juice and pulse till smooth.
- Through a strainer, strain the mixture, pressing with the back of a spatula.
- Fill 2 large glasses with the ice and top with the strained grape liquid.
- Pour the soda water on top evenly and serve immediately.

Amount per serving: 2

Timing Information:

Preparation	5 mins
Total Time	5 mins

Nutritional Information:

Calories	176.4
Fat	0.2g
Cholesterol	0.0mg
Sodium	41.0mg
Carbohydrates	46.3g
Protein	0.9g

* Percent Daily Values are based on a 2,000 calorie diet.

ITALIAN MEATBALLS IN GRAPE JELLY SAUCE

Ingredients

- 3 -5 lbs frozen cooked small meatballs
- 1 (32 oz.) jars grape jelly
- 2 (12 oz.) jars chili sauce
- 1 pinch cayenne pepper

Directions

- In a pan, mix together the chili sauce, grape jelly and cayenne pepper and stir in the meatballs.
- Simmer for about 45 minutes.

Amount per serving: 1

Timing Information:

Preparation	10 mins
Total Time	55 mins

Nutritional Information:

Calories	61.8
Fat	0.0g
Cholesterol	0.0mg
Sodium	187.4mg
Carbohydrates	15.2g
Protein	0.3g

* Percent Daily Values are based on a 2,000 calorie diet.

CLASSIC FALL GRAPE DINNER

Ingredients

- 1 butternut squash, peeled and cut into 1 1/2 inch pieces
- 1 1/2 C. red seedless grapes
- 1 medium onion, cut into 1 inch pieces
- 1 tbsp fresh sage, sliced into thin ribbons
- 1 tbsp olive oil
- 2 tbsp unsalted butter, melted
- salt and pepper
- 1/4 C. pine nuts, toasted

Directions

- Set your oven to 425 degrees F before doing anything else.
- In a large bowl, add all the ingredients and toss to coat well.
- Transfer the mixture in a large rimmed baking dish and cook everything in the oven for about 50 minutes.

Amount per serving: 4

Timing Information:

Preparation	20 mins
Total Time	1 hr 10 mins

Nutritional Information:

Calories	316.8
Fat	15.3g
Cholesterol	15.2mg
Sodium	14.6mg
Carbohydrates	47.4g
Protein	4.8g

* Percent Daily Values are based on a 2,000 calorie diet.

ITALIAN STYLE PIZZA

Ingredients

- 16 oz. premade pizza dough
- 1/2 C. Tomato Pasta Sauce, creamy mozzarella sauce
- 1/2 C. shredded whole milk mozzarella
- 1/2 C. shredded provolone cheese
- 1/4 C. goat cheese, crumbled
- 1/4 C. pine nuts
- 10 red grapes, halved
- 1/4 C. arugula, finely chopped
- 1 tbsp dried rosemary leaves
- 1 tbsp dried oregano
- 1/2 tsp dried cilantro

Directions

- Set your oven to 475 degrees F before doing anything else and grease a baking sheet.
- Arrange the pizza dough ball onto the prepared baking sheet and flatten the center of the dough thinly.
- The crust should be 12-14-inches in diameter.

- In a bowl, mix together tomato sauce, arugula, cilantro and oregano.
- Spread the sauce mixture over the dough evenly.
- Place the mozzarella and provolone cheeses over the sauce evenly.
- Top with the grapes, followed by rosemary, goat cheese and pine nuts.
- Cook everything in the oven for about 11-14 minutes.

Amount per serving: 4

Timing Information:

Preparation	20 mins
Total Time	33 mins

Nutritional Information:

Calories	379.2
Fat	13.9g
Cholesterol	22.4mg
Sodium	239.8mg
Carbohydrates	59.9g
Protein	10.9g

* Percent Daily Values are based on a 2,000 calorie diet.

NUTRITIOUS GRAPE SMOOTHIE

Ingredients

- 1 C. purple grapes
- 1 banana
- 1/2 C. orange juice

Directions

- In a blender, add all the ingredients and pulse till smooth.
- Serve immediately.

Amount per serving: 1

Timing Information:

Preparation	5 mins
Total Time	5 mins

Nutritional Information:

Calories	271.2
Fat	0.8g
Cholesterol	0.0mg
Sodium	5.6mg
Carbohydrates	68.8g
Protein	3.3g

* Percent Daily Values are based on a 2,000 calorie diet.

FAMILY FEAST BAKED GRAPE

Ingredients

- 4 eggs, beaten
- 200 g reduced-fat honey yogurt
- 1 tsp vanilla essence
- 3 tsp cornflour
- 500 g crimson seedless grapes
- 2 tbsp almonds, toasted

Directions

- Set your oven to 350 degrees F before doing anything else.
- In a bowl, add the beaten eggs, yogurt, corn flour and vanilla essence and beat till smooth.
- In a baking dish, place half of the grapes and top with the eggs mixture evenly.
- Place the remaining grapes over the yogurt mixture evenly.
- Cook everything in the oven for about 30 minutes.
- Remove everything from the oven and sprinkle with brown sugar and the almonds evenly.
- Keep aside to cool slightly.
- Serve warm.

Amount per serving: 4

Timing Information:

Preparation	10 mins
Total Time	40 mins

Nutritional Information:

Calories	192.0
Fat	7.1g
Cholesterol	186.0mg
Sodium	87.7mg
Carbohydrates	25.4g
Protein	8.1g

* Percent Daily Values are based on a 2,000 calorie diet.

Grapes Cooling Treat

(Granita)

Ingredients

- 3 C. green seedless grapes
- 2 tbsp apple juice
- 1 lime, juice of
- 1 fresh mint leaves (optional)

Directions

- In a blender, add all the ingredients and pulse till smooth.
- Transfer the mixture into a shallow baking dish and freeze for about 1-2 hours.
- Remove everything from the freezer and with a fork, break the granita into pieces.
- Transfer the granita into a blender and blend well.
- Serve immediately with a garnishing of the lime wedge.

Amount per serving: 4

Timing Information:

Preparation	5 mins
Total Time	4 hrs 5 mins

Nutritional Information:

Calories	88.6
Fat	0.2g
Cholesterol	0.0mg
Sodium	2.8mg
Carbohydrates	23.3g
Protein	0.9g

* Percent Daily Values are based on a 2,000 calorie diet.

ENGLISH GRAPE-NUT BREAD

Ingredients

- 2/3 C. plain yogurt
- 1 3/4 C. milk
- 2 C. Grape-nuts cereal
- 1 C. rolled oats
- 2/3 C. honey
- 2 tsp salt
- 3 -4 C. bread flour
- 2 tbsp instant yeast
- 1 tbsp canola oil
- flour, for dusting work surface

Directions

- In a large bowl, add the milk and yogurt and mix till smooth.
- Stir in the grape nut cereal and keep aside for about 15-20 minutes.
- Add the oats, honey and salt and mix till well combined.
- Slowly, add 1 C. of the flour and mix till well combined.
- Add the yeast and mix well.

- Slowly, add the remaining flour about 1/2 C. at one time and mix till a thick mixture forms.
- Transfer the mixture onto a floured surface and knead till a sticky dough forms.
- Grease a bowl with the oil and roll the dough in the bowl evenly.
- Cover the bowl and keep it at a warm place for about 90 minutes.
- With your hands, punch down the dough and keep it aside for several minutes.
- Divide the dough in 2 equal sized loaves.
- With plastic wrap, cover the loaves and keep it in a warm place for about 50 minutes.
- Set your oven to 350 degrees F.
- Cook everything in the oven for 25-35 minutes

Amount per serving: 24

Timing Information:

Preparation	30 mins
Total Time	2 hrs 30 mins

Nutritional Information:

Calories	156.8
Fat	2.0g
Cholesterol	3.3mg
Sodium	265.9mg
Carbohydrates	31.3g
Protein	4.4g

* Percent Daily Values are based on a 2,000 calorie diet.

REFRESHING GRAPE DRINK

Ingredients

- 1 oz. vodka
- 2 oz. grape juice
- 1/2 oz. cranberry juice cocktail
- 1/2 oz. pineapple juice
- ice

Directions

- In a bowl, add all the ingredients and shake well.
- Strain into a glass and add the ice.
- Serve immediately.

Amount per serving: 1

Timing Information:

Preparation	5 mins
Total Time	5 mins

Nutritional Information:

Calories	119.2
Fat	0.0g
Cholesterol	0.0mg
Sodium	2.5mg
Carbohydrates	12.2g
Protein	0.3g

* Percent Daily Values are based on a 2,000 calorie diet.

FRENCH GRAPE PIZZA

Ingredients

- 1 thin pizza crust
- 2 C. red grapes, sliced in half
- 1/2 lb Italian sausage, browned and crumbled
- 6 oz. fresh goat cheese
- extra virgin olive oil
- salt and pepper

Directions

- Set your oven to 450 degrees F before doing anything else.
- Arrange the pizza crust in a pizza pan.
- Brush the crust with the oil and sprinkle with salt and black pepper.
- Place the sausage over the pizza crust, followed by the grapes and goat cheese.
- Cook everything in the oven for about 13-15 minutes.

Amount per serving: 2

Timing Information:

Preparation	5 mins
Total Time	20 mins

Nutritional Information:

Calories	804.7
Fat	56.6g
Cholesterol	132.0mg
Sodium	1811.7mg
Carbohydrates	34.3g
Protein	41.1g

* Percent Daily Values are based on a 2,000 calorie diet.

Delicious Summertime Salsa

Ingredients

- 2 C. green seedless grapes, quartered
- 2 C. red seedless grapes, quartered
- 1 English cucumber, peeled and chopped
- 1 sweet onion, finely chopped
- 1 bunch cilantro, finely chopped
- 3 -4 finely chopped jalapeno peppers
- 1/2 fresh lime, squeezed on top
- 1/4 tsp salt
- tortilla chips

Directions

- In a large bowl, mix together all the ingredients and refrigerate, covered for at least 1 hour.

Amount per serving: 1

Timing Information:

Preparation	20 mins
Total Time	20 mins

Nutritional Information:

Calories	187.5
Fat	0.6g
Cholesterol	0.0mg
Sodium	206.1mg
Carbohydrates	48.3g
Protein	3.0g

* Percent Daily Values are based on a 2,000 calorie diet.

FAMILY FAVORITE DRINK

Ingredients

- ice
- 3 C. white grape juice
- 1/2 C. lemon juice
- 2 C. carbonated lemon-lime beverage
- 1 bunch grapes, washed and halved
- 1 lemon, sliced into rounds

Directions

- Fill a large pitcher with the ice.
- Add both the juices and beverage and gently stir to combine.
- Divide the mixture in the serving glasses and serve with a garnishing of the grapes and lemon wedges.

Amount per serving: 1

Timing Information:

Preparation	10 mins
Total Time	10 mins

Nutritional Information:

Calories	1874.2
Fat	3.4g
Cholesterol	0.0mg
Sodium	109.7mg
Carbohydrates	469.9g
Protein	7.8g

* Percent Daily Values are based on a 2,000 calorie diet.

GORGEOUS DINNER MEAL

Ingredients

- 2 lbs carrots, small, whole with tops
- 4 sprigs fresh rosemary, 4 6-inch sprigs
- salt, to taste
- 2 tbsp butter
- 1/3 C. wild grape and port jelly

Directions

- Trim and peel the carrots, then cut them in half lengthwise.
- In a large Dutch oven, add the carrots with the rosemary sprigs and salt.
- Add enough water to cover the carrots and bring to a boil.
- Reduce the heat and simmer, covered for about 8-10 minutes.
- Drain well and discard the rosemary sprigs.
- In the same Dutch oven, melt the butter and add the carrots and toss to coat.
- Transfer the carrots into serving plates and top with the jelly and serve.

Amount per serving: 8

Timing Information:

Preparation	30 mins
Total Time	38 mins

Nutritional Information:

Calories	72.1
Fat	3.1g
Cholesterol	7.6mg
Sodium	98.9mg
Carbohydrates	10.9g
Protein	1.0g

* Percent Daily Values are based on a 2,000 calorie diet.

SUMMERTIME GRAPE TREAT

Ingredients

- 1 1/2 C. red seedless grapes, cut in half
- 4 1/2 C. white grape juice

Directions

- Place the grape halves into the pop molds evenly and pour the grape juice on top.
- Freeze everything for about 1 1/2-2 hours, then insert the sticks.
- Freeze for 6 hours more.
- Remove the pops from the molds and serve immediately.

Amount per serving: 6

Timing Information:

Preparation	10 mins
Total Time	16 mins

Nutritional Information:

Calories	412.6
Fat	0.7g
Cholesterol	0.0mg
Sodium	15.8mg
Carbohydrates	102.6g
Protein	1.6g

* Percent Daily Values are based on a 2,000 calorie diet.

HEALTHY LUNCHEON GRAPE WRAPS

Ingredients

- 1 (12 inch) flour tortillas, warmed
- 1/3 C. red seedless California grapes, halved
- 2 oz. grilled chicken breasts, sliced
- 1 tbsp creamy Caesar salad dressing
- 1 C. romaine lettuce, cut
- 1 tbsp creamy Caesar salad dressing
- 1 tbsp parmesan cheese, shredded
- croutons

Directions

- Place the tortilla onto a large plate.
- Arrange all the ingredients over tortilla in the layers of grapes, chicken, 1 tsp of dressing, lettuce, remaining dressing, cheese and croutons.
- Fold the lower third of the tortilla around the filling and fold the outer edges inward to close the end and roll like a cylinder.

Amount per serving: 1

Timing Information:

Preparation	5 mins
Total Time	5 mins

Nutritional Information:

Calories	579.2
Fat	27.1g
Cholesterol	64.0mg
Sodium	1012.8mg
Carbohydrates	54.9g
Protein	28.0g

* Percent Daily Values are based on a 2,000 calorie diet.

CALIFORNIAN GRAPE SANDWICH

Ingredients

- 1 C. coarsely chopped seedless grapes
- 1 C. canned corn kernel
- 1/4 C. chopped onion
- 1 garlic clove, minced
- 2 tbsp chopped cilantro
- 1/3 C. bottled low-fat Italian salad dressing
- 1 C. shredded lowfat mozzarella cheese
- 1 loaf focaccia bread, sliced in half horizontally
- 1 lb cooked chicken breast

Directions

- Set your grill to medium heat.
- In a bowl, mix together the grapes, onion, corn, garlic, cilantro and salad dressing.
- Place about 1/2 C. of the cheese over the bottom half of the bread and top with the chicken evenly.
- Place 1 C. of the grape mixture over the chicken evenly and top with the remaining cheese.

- With foil wrap the sandwich and cook it on the grill for about 5 minutes.
- Unwrap the sandwich and cut into 4 desired size portions.
- Serve these sandwiches with the remaining grape mixture.

Amount per serving: 4

Timing Information:

Preparation	5 mins
Total Time	15 mins

Nutritional Information:

Calories	309.9
Fat	10.4g
Cholesterol	96.4mg
Sodium	356.5mg
Carbohydrates	18.5g
Protein	35.6g

* Percent Daily Values are based on a 2,000 calorie diet.

Grape Coleslaw for Celebration Days

Ingredients

- 1/4 C. apple cider vinegar
- 1/2 tsp ground ginger
- 1/4 tsp ground cardamom
- 1/4 tsp black pepper
- 1/2 tsp poppy seed
- 1 tbsp honey
- 1/3 C. olive oil

- 1 tsp fresh lavender flowers
- 10 oz. thinly sliced cabbage
- 2 thinly scallions
- 1/2 C. sliced seedless grapes
- 1/2 C. toasted sliced almonds
- 1/3 C. crushed apple chips

Directions

- In a bowl, add all the dressing ingredients and beat till well combined.
- In another bowl, mix together the salad ingredients.
- Add the dressing and toss to coat well.
- Refrigerate for about 1 hour before serving.

Amount per serving: 6

Timing Information:

Preparation	10 mins
Total Time	10 mins

Nutritional Information:

Calories	187.4
Fat	16.0g
Cholesterol	0.0mg
Sodium	10.6mg
Carbohydrates	10.1g
Protein	2.5g

* Percent Daily Values are based on a 2,000 calorie diet.

Colorful Fruit Salad

Ingredients

- 1 1/2 C. cantaloupe, shaped into balls
- 1 1/2 C. watermelon, shaped into balls
- 1 1/2 C. green grapes
- Dressing
- 1/4 C. orange juice
- 1 tbsp honey
- 1 tbsp lime juice
- 2 tsp jalapenos, minced
- 1/2 tsp lime peel, grated

Directions

- In a sealable bag, add all the ingredients and seal the bag tightly.
- Shake till well combined and refrigerate for about 1 hour.

Amount per serving: 6

Timing Information:

Preparation	15 mins
Total Time	1 hr 15 mins

Nutritional Information:

Calories	67.1
Fat	0.2g
Cholesterol	0.0mg
Sodium	7.8mg
Carbohydrates	17.1g
Protein	0.9g

* Percent Daily Values are based on a 2,000 calorie diet.

Armenian Grape Pilaf

Ingredients

- 1 C. long grain white rice
- 1 medium onion, sliced thinly
- 1 garlic clove, minced
- 8 chicken thighs
- 2 tbsp vegetable oil
- 1/2 tsp cinnamon
- 1/2 tsp sugar
- 2 C. chicken stock
- salt and pepper
- 1 lb red seedless grapes

Directions

- Set your oven to 375 degrees F before doing anything else.
- Place the rice in the bottom of a large casserole dish.
- In a large skillet, heat the oil on medium heat and cook the chicken thighs for about 2-3 minutes per side.
- Transfer the chicken thighs over the rice into a casserole dish.
- In the same skillet, add the onion and sauté for about 5 minutes.

- Stir in the garlic, sugar and cinnamon and sauté for few seconds and transfer the mixture over the chicken.
- In the skillet, add the broth and stir to scrape the brown bits.
- Pour the broth on top of the casserole dish and sprinkle with the salt and black pepper.
- Cover and cook everything in the oven for about 1 hour.
- Remove the chicken thighs from the casserole dish and stir the remaining mixture to combine.
- Place the chicken over the rice mixture and cook, covered in the oven for about 10 minutes.

Amount per serving: 6

Timing Information:

Preparation	20 mins
Total Time	1 hr 45 mins

Nutritional Information:

Calories	508.0
Fat	24.9g
Cholesterol	107.6mg
Sodium	213.5mg
Carbohydrates	43.5g
Protein	26.6g

* Percent Daily Values are based on a 2,000 calorie diet.

FLAVORFUL GRAPE CHUTNEY

Ingredients

- 4 C. red seedless grapes
- 1 tbsp butter
- 1/2 C. chopped red onion
- 1 tsp fresh rosemary, snipped
- 1/4 tsp dried oregano, crumbled
- 2 tbsp balsamic vinegar

Directions

- In a food processor, add the grapes and pulse till chopped finely.
- In a large skillet, melt the butter and sauté the onion for about 5 minutes.
- Stir in the herbs and sauté for about 1 minute.
- Stir in the vinegar and chopped grapes and cook for about 1-2 minutes.
- Serve immediately.

Amount per serving: 1

Timing Information:

Preparation	10 mins
Total Time	20 mins

Nutritional Information:

Calories	24.1
Fat	0.5g
Cholesterol	1.2mg
Sodium	4.0mg
Carbohydrates	5.1g
Protein	0.2g

* Percent Daily Values are based on a 2,000 calorie diet.

Grape Tarts for Thanksgiving

Ingredients

- 1 sheet frozen reduced-fat puff pastry, thawed
- 2/3 C. low-fat ricotta cheese
- 1 tbsp honey
- 1.5 C. thompson seedless grapes
- 2 tsp sugar
- 1/4 C. walnuts, chopped

Directions

- Set your oven to 425 degrees F before doing anything else and line a baking dish with parchment paper.
- Cut the pastry sheet into 4 squares and then cut about 1/2-inch border around the edge of each square.
- Place the pastry squares into a prepared baking dish.
- In a bowl, mix together the honey and ricotta cheese.
- Spread the honey mixture over each pastry square leaving the border and top with the grapes.
- Sprinkle with the sugar and walnuts and cook everything in the oven till golden.

Amount per serving: 4

Timing Information:

Preparation	12 mins
Total Time	27 mins

Nutritional Information:

Calories	541.5
Fat	1.2g
Cholesterol	0.0mg
Sodium	15.2mg
Carbohydrates	142.1g
Protein	5.4g

* Percent Daily Values are based on a 2,000 calorie diet.

THANKS FOR READING! NOW LET'S TRY SOME **SUSHI** AND **DUMP DINNERS**....

http://bit.ly/2443TFg

To grab this **box set** simply follow the link mentioned above, or tap the book cover.

This will take you to a page where you can simply enter your email address and a PDF version of the **box set** will be emailed to you.

I hope you are ready for some serious cooking!

http://bit.ly/2443TFg

You will also receive updates about all my new books when they are free.

Also don't forget to like and subscribe on the social networks. I love meeting my readers. Links to all my profiles are below so please click and connect :)

Facebook

Twitter

COME ON...
LET'S BE FRIENDS :)

I adore my readers and love connecting with them socially. Please follow the links below so we can connect on Facebook, Twitter, and Google+.

Facebook

Twitter

I also have a blog that I regularly update for my readers so check it out below.

My Blog

CAN I ASK A FAVOUR?

If you found this book interesting, or have otherwise found any benefit in it. Then may I ask that you post a review of it on Amazon? Nothing excites me more than new reviews, especially reviews which suggest new topics for writing. I do read all reviews and I always factor feedback into my newer works.

So if you are willing to take ten minutes to write what you sincerely thought about this book then please visit our Amazon page and post your opinions.

Again thank you!

INTERESTED IN OTHER EASY COOKBOOKS?

Everything is easy! Check out my Amazon Author page for more great cookbooks:

For a complete listing of all my books please see my author page.

46081520R00066

Made in the USA
Middletown, DE
21 July 2017